DATE DUE

BEARS
and their forest cousins

ANIMAL FAMILIES

BEARS
and their forest cousins

Annemarie Schmidt and Christian R. Schmidt

Gareth Stevens Children's Books
MILWAUKEE

A N I M A L   F A M I L I E S

For a free color catalog describing Gareth Stevens' list of high-quality children's books, call 1-800-341-3569 (USA) or 1-800-461-9120 (Canada).

Picture Credits
Color illustrations are from Jacana (Switzerland) and Paris, with the exception of the following: C. Anzenberger — 10 (2. series/2); Comet-Photo — 9; Historical Museum, Bern — 8; J. Jelinek — 7; Kinderbuchverlag Luzern-Jin Xuqi — 10 (4. series/1), 28; Jurg Klages — 12, 19; Robert Maier — 11, 32 (also 10, 5. series/1); Okapia — 6 (Tom McHugh), 10 (5. series/4 — R. Hofels), 22 (S. Nagendra); Ivo Poglayen-Neuwall — 33 (right), 34, 35 (also 10, 6. series/1); Chr. R. Schmidt — title page, 10 (1. series/3), 15 (also 10, 1. series/4), 17, 18, 20, 23, 27, 30, 33 (left) (also 10, 5. series/2); WGS/ Steiff — 40; Zoological Society of San Diego/Mark Rich — (2. series/4).

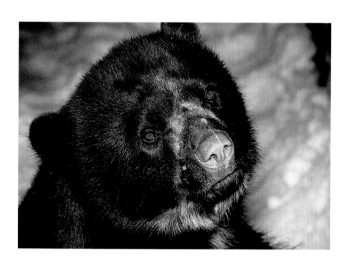

Library of Congress Cataloging-in-Publication Data

Schmidt, Annemarie.
    [Bären. English]
    Bears and their forest cousins / Annemarie Schmidt and Christian
R. Schmidt.
        p. cm. — (Animal families)
    Translation of: Bären.
    "North American edition"—T.p. verso.
    Includes bibliographical references and index.
    Summary: Presents an evolutional and historical accounting of the bear
family, as well as the physical attributes, life expectancies, native
environments, and daily habits of its major members.
    ISBN 0-8368-0684-0
    1. Bears—Juvenile literature. 2. Procyonidae—Juvenile literature. 3.
Pandas—Juvenile literature. [1. Bears. 2. Procyonidae. 3. Pandas.] I.
Schmidt, Christian R. II. Title. III. Series: Animal families (Milwaukee, Wis.)
QL737.C27S2713 1991
599.74'446—dc20   91-9428

North American edition first published in 1991 by
Gareth Stevens Children's Books
1555 North RiverCenter Drive, Suite 201
Milwaukee, Wisconsin 53212, USA

Series editors: Amy Bauman and Patricia Lantier-Sampon
Editor: Barbara Behm
Designer: Sharone Burris
Translated from the German by: Jamie Daniel
Editorial assistants: Scott Enk, Diane Laska, and Andrea Schneider

Printed in MEXICO

4 5 6 7 8 9 96

Table of Contents

What Is a Bear? 7
A Guide to Bears
   and Their Forest Cousins 10
Brown Bears:
   The European Brown Bear ...11
   The Grizzly Bear 13
   The Kodiak Bear 15
   The Syrian Brown Bear 15
Black Bears:
   The American Black Bear 16
   The Cinnamon Bear 17
   The Glacier Bear 17
   The Kermode Bear 17
   The Polar Bear 18
   The Himalayan Black Bear ...20
   The Sloth Bear 22
   The Sun Bear 24
   The Spectacled Bear 26
Pandas:
   The Panda 28
   The Giant Panda 30
Raccoons:
   The Raccoon 32
   The Aquara 33
   The Cacomistle 33
   The Kinkajou 34
   The Olingo 35
   The Red Coati 36
   The Coati 37
The "Bear" That Isn't a Bear:
   The Koala 38
Every Child's Favorite:
   The Teddy Bear 40
Appendix 41

What Is a Bear?

To many people, bears symbolize the untouched wilderness, nature itself. To others, bears are sacred, filled with healing powers and spiritual forces. Bears have many faces, and each is unique and magnificent. Members of the bear family can be very different. They can be large or small, shaggy or smooth-coated, black, brown, or white, gentle or frightening. This book will help you get better acquainted with the powerful and exciting bear family. It will also acquaint you with other animals that are related to bears or have some qualities, physical or otherwise, that are similar to those of bears.

About thirty to forty million years ago, bears began to evolve from a family of small mammals called miacids. The oldest known bear was about as large as a medium-sized dog and lived in Europe about twenty million years ago. Today's bears developed from a little bear known as Protursus.

People have always considered bears to be special animals. In early times, the bear was often thought of as the "king of the beasts." People marveled at its strength and cleverness. Today, people still tell stories and fables about the bear. In many countries around the world, it has even been given nicknames. In Germany it's called "Master Bruin"; the Scandinavians call it "Bamse" or "Nalle," and Russian writers have baptized it "Mikhail Ivanovitch."

Many ancient peoples honored the bear. The giant cave bear, the forerunner of the brown bear, can be seen in cave paintings made tens of thousands of years ago. The bear has a special place in Scandinavia, northern Japan, and Siberia as well. Many peoples honored the female bear in particular — an outstanding mother who lovingly cares

Opposite: The trail of a Kodiak bear crosses the Alaskan landscape. Like people, bears walk on the soles of their feet. They also have five fingers on each front paw and five toes on each hind paw. Below: As early as four thousand years ago, bears were being shown in simple drawings. This is a drawing of a cave bear from a cave in Norway.

for her children — as a symbol of fertility and maternity. The bear even has a place in the heavens; the "Great Bear" is an important constellation in the northern sky.

The bear had a special place among the original inhabitants of the North American continent. Many North American Indians believed that the grizzly bear was every bit as clever as people and a favorite of Manitou, the Great Spirit. Many Indian tribes of the past referred to the grizzly as "Brother Bear." The warriors prayed to Manitou for forgiveness before going out to hunt bears.

In Europe, many small and large communities include a reference to the bear in their names. Bern, which is the capital of Switzerland, even has a bear pit where the living animal can be admired. Names of many places can also be traced back to bear caravans that were led across Europe two thousand years ago on the orders of the Roman caesars.

In those days, many bears were brought from northern European countries to Rome, where they were forced to fight in the ring with gladiators. In one instance, it is believed that four hundred bears were brought into an arena at the same time! Another story recounts that a Swiss bear helped the Irish monk Gallus gather firewood in the year A.D. 600. The cloister and city of St. Gallen in Ireland were later built on the spot where the fire supposedly burned.

Part of the reason bears have been popular for so long is probably that they have many similarities to people. Although the bear is a predator, it is not strictly a meat-eater. Like people, it also likes to eat plants, berries, and honey. The bear also walks on the soles of its feet. It can stand upright and walk on its hind feet, just like people.

In earlier times, bears were often exploited or abused by people. Bear "tamers" traveled across the country with their trained dancing bears and took money for the bears' performances. The public either did not know or did not care that the bears often had to "learn" how to dance by practicing on painful hot oven plates. In South America, the Indians even made bears operate devices called bellows that ignited huge work fires.

In many cases, people have moved bears out of their natural habitats in order to claim the land for themselves. People have also killed bears for their beautiful skins. As a result of such activities, the Atlas bear has been extinct for some time. European brown bears can now be found only in Scandinavia, eastern Europe, and, very infrequently, in southern Europe. The spectacled bear, sloth bears, and grizzlies haven't fared much better. The polar bear also came close to extinction but is now protected worldwide.

Conflicts develop periodically between tourists and the black bears and grizzlies in North America's national parks. Since people often feed them, the bears sometimes lose their natural passiveness and become dangerous. This is usually not the bear's fault. Rather, it is people who have caused the bear to change its natural behavior.

Bears are not malicious animals, but they are curious by nature. If something interests them, they usually want to investigate. If this something happens to be a human being, then the encounter can be unpleasant under certain circumstances. This curious nature is often complicated by the bear's mood, which is difficult for people to determine. Unlike cats, who hiss to give a clear indication that they are angry, bears remain without expression. Whether they are in a good or a

Left: In the state of Alaska, where bears can still live undisturbed, the state flag shows the North Star and the constellation of the "Great Bear." Below: Even today, bears are sometimes kept in bear pits, like this one in Bern, Switzerland.

mother in spring. Once out in the open, however, they adapt quickly to outside conditions and follow their natural instincts almost immediately. Cubs are very playful and curious; they remain under their mother's protection for up to three years. When they finally do become adults and leave their mother, they are well prepared for the outside world. They have been lovingly and carefully trained to be independent.

bad mood, their faces remain unchanged. A bear can be most dangerous if it is surprised. In this case, what looks like an attack is in reality only a defensive strategy — the bear is protecting itself against an intruder into its territory. Guides often advise hikers in North American national parks to take a bell along with them. This will give the bears roaming in the area plenty of advance warning.

Most bears live alone. They can be seen together only during mating season and when a female gives birth to her offspring. In cold climates, most big bears sleep, or hibernate, in winter. The bear's sleep, however, is not as deep as people often think. Bears are not true hibernators. They sometimes wake up and take a winter stroll before going back to their dens to fall asleep again. This happens especially when the bears get hungry, when they didn't put on enough fat in the previous fall to last the entire winter.

During the hibernation period, the female bear gives birth to her young. The cubs are very small and completely helpless at birth. They leave their safe den only with their

A Guide to
Bears and Their Forest Cousins

European brown bear

grizzly bear

Kodiak bear

Syrian brown bear

American black bear

cinnamon bear

glacier bear

Kermode bear

polar bear

Himalayan black bear

sloth bear

sun bear

spectacled bear

giant panda

panda

raccoon

aquara

cacomistle

kinkajou

olingo

red coati

coati

The Brown Bears

Weight: 155-750 pounds (70-340 kg)
Total length: 5.6-6.6 feet (1.7-2 m)

THE EUROPEAN BROWN BEAR

The brown bear is rare in Europe because people have hunted it for centuries. This has forced the brown bear out of its native regions, and into the last wilderness areas of Europe. Thus, there are still small numbers of the bears in the Pyrenees, the Alps, and the Abruzzis, and larger populations in northern and eastern Europe. The European brown bear is very gentle and content as long as it is left alone. It is extremely adaptable and feels at home on the coast and in the mountains, in the dense forest and in the open tundra. The size of a brown bear's territory depends on the amount of food available and on the gender of the individual bear. Male bears generally have territories that cover between 270 and 10,765 square feet (25-1,000 sq m). Females have smaller areas, between 160 and 2,155 square feet (15-200 sq m).

A European brown bear stands contentedly in his mountain habitat.

A brown bear patiently nurses her three cubs.

Brown bears' sense of smell is approximately 100,000 times more sensitive than that of humans. This helps them search for food. As omnivores, they eat more plants than anything else, but they also eat insect larvae, rodents, and fish. Honey and honeycombs of wild bees provide a special treat. The brown bear eats up to 26 pounds (12 kg) of food daily.

When the European brown bear begins hibernation in October or November, it moves into a protected spot. This is usually a hollow tree or a private den that it has dug out to sleep in through the cold season. Food is scarce during winter because of snow.

The bears' mating season is in spring. Male bears often fight over females during this time. The cubs don't begin to grow inside the mother's body right away, but, rather, in autumn, when she is hibernating. This is why most brown bear cubs are born during January. The female usually gives birth to two to four cubs. They are very tiny at first and covered with only a fine fuzz. After a month, the cubs finally open their eyes. When they leave the den in April or May with their mother for the first time, they are about as big as half-grown German shepherd dogs and just as playful. Brown bears live to be twenty to thirty years old.

THE GRIZZLY BEAR

The North American grizzly is a well known brown bear. It gets its name from the grizzled, or gray, fur that often shimmers across its shoulders and on its back. But this name is often misleading, since the coloring of these bears varies. The grizzly bears in one region often have bright, light-colored coats, while their cousins in another will be dark. The grizzly is even more of a loner than other bears and is easily excited. If it attacks, it can reach a speed of about 30 miles (50 km) per hour, and is not nearly as clumsy as it might appear at first glance. People often run into problems with grizzlies because people are often reckless or unfamiliar with the bears' habits. Like all bears, grizzlies cannot see or hear very well. As a result, there are often unexpected "close encounters" between grizzlies and people in national parks. In these cases, people have usually gotten too close to the bears. The bears attack out of necessity. Attacks are most often made by mother bears who are concerned for the safety of their young.

Grizzlies like to hunt for their food more than any of the other brown bears. But they also like plants. Grizzlies have also been known to eat livestock near human settlements. Their jaws have from thirty-four to forty-two teeth, with 1-inch- (2.5-cm-) long canine teeth and rounded molars. The grizzly's bite is well suited for a varied diet.

In addition to fearing people, the grizzly also has reason to fear wolves. If a mother grizzly is attacked by a pack of wolves, she will drive her cubs — who are agile climbers — toward a tree, where the cubs can climb up to safety. She will do the same thing if a male bear comes too close to the cubs. This is in most cases a wise decision because male bears often harm innocent cubs. Like many other bears, the grizzly bear has been forced into more remote areas because it is hunted by people.

A pair of grizzly bears stand up on their hind legs to fight.

THE KODIAK BEAR

The Kodiak bear is the largest land predator on earth. It is at home on the southern coast of Alaska and on several neighboring islands, as well as on Kodiak Island in the Gulf of Alaska. The coat of this powerful bear is usually a golden brown, but it can sometimes be quite dark. More slender and long-legged than the grizzly, the Kodiak can reach a total length of 10 feet (3 m) and weigh from 1,100 to 1,650 pounds (500-750 kg). When standing on its hind legs, it is easily 10 feet (3 m) tall! The male bears usually weigh 1.5 times as much as the females. This can come in handy when the males are fighting against rivals for the attentions of the females. The males sharpen their ivory-colored claws, which can reach 2.5 inches (6 cm) in length, on trees. They reach up as high as possible into the trees and scratch the trunks until their claws are razor-sharp. The male bears also spray themselves with urine and rub scent marks with their shoulder fur onto the trees in the surrounding area. These are signs for the females that a male bear is ready to mate. At the same time, this warns rivals that someone else is already the "lord of the manor" in this area.

Once a year, the Kodiak bear forgets that it is a loner. When the salmon come back from the sea to their spawning grounds, the Kodiaks gather together along the rivers in order to take advantage of nature's abundance. It is an unforgettable sight to observe the powerful bears pulling huge quantities of fish from the swiftly moving water. While one bear leaps comically into the water to catch its food, others fish for the salmon with subtle swipes of their large paws. Still another bear waits patiently along the edge of the river until a fish actually springs right into its mouth! When the annual salmon run is over, the Kodiak bears return to their usual meals of plants.

THE SYRIAN BROWN BEAR

The various brown bears have the greatest territorial range of all the bears. Approximately 250,000 years ago, brown bears crossed Europe from their home base in Asia. About 50,000 years ago, brown bears succeeded in

Above: This Syrian brown bear has a glossy, silvery brown coat.
Opposite: Kodiak bears catch fish in the annual salmon run.

crossing over into the New World by way of the stretch of land that connected Siberia and the Americas at that time.

The smallest of these bears is the Syrian brown bear, which lives in southeastern Asia. This bear's coat is brighter than that of most of its cousins', and it has noticeably larger ears. Like the Alp bear, of which only thirty animals at most survive, the Syrian brown bear is rare. It has been fiercely pursued and forced back into desolate mountainous areas by people because it occasionally attacks livestock. But these same people have claimed the bears' natural habitats for their own settlements and fields.

The Black Bears

Weight: 155-640 pounds (70-290 kg)
Total length: 4-6 feet (1.3-1.8 m)

Two black bear cubs climb quickly up a tree to safety while their mother stands guard below.

THE AMERICAN BLACK BEAR

Bears have always commanded the respect of American Indians. The Cree and Atabask, for example, believed that the American black bear was very intelligent and a born leader. But in contests with its larger relative, the grizzly, this leadership quality is of little use to the American black bear. The grizzly is simply much more powerful. As a rule, the American black bear tries to avoid its cousin.

But the American black bear outranks the grizzly bear in one area. It seems to have a much better understanding of how to adapt to people than its relative. This is apparent because, in contrast to the grizzly, the American black bear can still be found from one end of the North American continent to the other — from the Pacific Coast to the Atlantic. Its main habitat is the forest, and adult black bears as well as their young are excellent climbers. Here in the woods they find the 11 to 18 pounds (5-8 kg) of food they need every day. They often eat tubers, roots, buds, berries, and honey, as well as worms, insects, caterpillars, fish, and small mammals.

Male black bears live in territories that cover anywhere from 6 to 230 square miles (15-600 sq km), while females live in smaller areas ranging from 1 to 36 square miles (3-94 sq km). Less food is available to the bears in western North America than eastern North America, so black bear territories in the West are larger. As a further adaptation to limited food supplies, the black bears in western North America have remained smaller in size.

American black bears hibernate for periods of 5 to 7.5 months in colder northern regions. In the southern regions, only pregnant females take a winter nap. After a gestation period of 210 to 215 days, they give birth to one to four cubs. The cubs will nurse for six or seven months and will remain with their mother for 1.5 to 2.5 years. They are ready to mate when they are between three and eight years of age.

The oldest American black bear on record lived to a ripe old age of thirty-two. Not every bear's life is so long, though, since they are still hunted by people.

THE CINNAMON BEAR, GLACIER BEAR, AND KERMODE BEAR

A bear cannot always be identified by its name. The designation *black bear* doesn't necessarily mean that a bear is black in color. There are eighteen kinds of bears called "black bears," but not all of them are black. For instance, there are reddish brown black bears in the western United States and the Canadian Rockies. They are referred to as cinnamon bears because of the color of their coats.

Farther northwest, in the border areas of Alaska, British Columbia, and the Yukon, is the home of small black bears known as blue glacier bears. Their shimmering, bluish gray coats may be an adaptation to the gray granite walls of their mountain homes. These bears also have a color similar to the ice of the area they inhabit. This makes them difficult to spot. It is hard to estimate just how many glacier bears exist in this wild, rugged habitat, but their numbers probably do not amount to more than several hundred.

The discovery of another color difference in the black bear family was made in November 1900. William T. Hornaday, the director of the Bronx Zoo in New York City, found a cream-colored black bear pelt by accident. He found the pelt at a Canadian fur dealer's store in Victoria, British Columbia. With the help of Francis Kermode, the director of the province's museum in Victoria, Hornaday acquired four more pelts. After careful examination, naturalists were convinced that they were in the presence of a new species. Hornaday named this "white black bear" the Kermode bear in 1905 after Francis Kermode. These bears are found only in a narrow stretch along the coast of British Columbia and on several of the adjacent islands. Their claws are white and their coats cream-colored and often dusted by a golden shimmer. The Kermodes have

A pair of blue glacier bears wrestle playfully with each other.

brown irises and grayish beige noses. Kermode cubs will be white only if both parents are white Kermode bears. In many litters, white and black Kermode siblings can be found together. Although they were once hunted as trophies, the Kermode bears are now protected by law.

The Polar Bear

Weight: 550-1,550 pounds (250-700 kg)
Total length: 6-10 feet (1.8-3 m)

Above: A young polar bear has fun swimming in cold Arctic waters.
Opposite: A mother polar bear sits contentedly feeding her cubs.

Polar bears live on the drifting ice and in the open sea around the North Pole. They are extremely well adapted to this harsh, frozen climate. Little webs on their feet and a streamlined body make them good, steady swimmers. They also like to dive underwater, although they won't stay under for more than two minutes at one time. A layer of fat under the skin protects polar bears against the cold, as does a thick, water-resistant coat. Their fur is a bright white color that helps to store heat and provide camouflage. Polar bears are relatively small members of the bear family, and their small limbs reduce the danger of freezing in their icy environment. Polar bears also have fur that partly covers the soles of their feet. This is an added feature that helps keep them warm.

Although many people once thought that polar bears moved in long, circular journeys around the pole, scientists now know that most of them remain in a certain area. But individual bears are still capable of traveling huge distances. One Alaskan polar bear was tagged and closely tracked by researchers. In one year it covered an astonishing distance of 695 miles (1,119 km)!

The polar bear's prey includes various types of seals that it never attacks in the water. Instead, it attacks when they come onto land to shed. The bear can hear the seals through breathing holes in the ice, and its keen sense of smell can detect the seals through 10 feet (3 m) of snow. In emergencies, the bear will also eat berries, birds, birds' eggs, lemmings, and other mammals.

Male polar bears are ready to mate when they are eight years old, and females when they are four or five. Polar bear cubs are born during the winter hibernation period. In November or December, pregnant polar bears dig out a den in a sloping coastline and allow themselves to be snowed in. They usually give birth to one or two cubs. Studies show that even when the temperatures outside sink to well below freezing, temperatures in the narrow den do not drop below freezing. When the cubs leave the den in spring, they weigh about 22 pounds (10 kg). They nurse for twenty-one months and leave their mother only at twenty-eight months of age.

Next to the parasitic larvae of the tapeworm, people are the polar bear's only other enemy. In 1956, the Soviet Union became the first country to legally protect the polar bear. When other countries followed this example in 1973, there were only about ten thousand polar bears left. Thanks to a worldwide effort to protect them, the numbers of polar bears are once again on the rise. In fact, people who live in the Arctic are now allowed to do a limited amount of polar-bear hunting.

The Himalayan Black Bear

Weight: 100-330 pounds (45-150 kg)
Total length: 4.3-5.6 feet (1.3-1.7 m)

Himalayan black bear cubs watch the world below from their sturdy perch high in the treetops.

The Himalayan black bear has a smooth coat in either deep black or dark gray. It also has a yellow, Y-shaped mark across its chest, and long hair that forms a thick collar around its throat and along the sides of its neck and shoulders. Big ears indicate that the Himalayan black bear can hear well, and its eyesight is better than that of any other kind of bear. The natural habitat of the Himalayan black bear extends from northern India across China and as far east as Japan. It prefers to live in remote mountain forests and along steep slopes with dense growths of rhododendron bushes.

The Himalayan black bear is an excellent swimmer and an expert climber that can climb to altitudes as high as 13,000 feet (4,000 m) in the summer. Its thick coat and warm undercoat protect it from cold and wind. In winter, though, life in the high mountains is too harsh even for the Himalayan black bear. Therefore, it climbs down to the valleys below for protection.

Himalayan black bears can climb trees with the same skill that they use to climb steep mountain cliffs. They build sleeping platforms with branches and twigs in the forks or hollows of trees. Because of the cold and the scarcity of food in cold weather, Himalayan black bears that live in the northern sections of their territorial range hibernate in winter. They hibernate in trees or in caves in the rocks. This is where pregnant bears give birth to one or two cubs. These babies will remain with their mother until spring. Each mother cares for her cubs for a period of two years. Himalayan black bears, just like other black bears, adapt easily to their surroundings, and they frequently venture close to the edges of human settlements. They are rather shy, however, and prefer to avoid people.

Experts are not sure what Himalayan black bears eat. Some describe the bears as herbivores that supplement their diet of acorns, fruit, nuts, tree bark, and corn with ants, insect larvae, and birds. Others believe that Himalayan black bears are carnivores that hunt deer, mountain sheep, and even livestock animals. It is possible, however, that Himalayan black bears adapt their eating habits to their particular location and whatever foods happen to be available.

As with other bears, Himalayan black bears occasionally have problems with people if they make themselves too obvious in corn-fields or livestock-grazing areas. Aside from people, however, their only enemies are tigers and wolves.

Opposite: An adult Himalayan black bear sits up-right and relaxes in an open field.

The Sloth Bear

Weight: 130-300 pounds (60-135 kg)
Total length: 4.6-6.2 feet (1.4-1.9 m)

A sloth bear sniffs the air eagerly.

Southern Nepal, India, and Sri Lanka are home for the sloth bear. It has a small body and long, shaggy fur that forms a thick mane around its throat and shoulders.

The sloth bear moves slowly and walks on long, curved claws. It lives alone or in pairs in wooded flatland areas. Most of the time, it stays on the ground, although it is an expert climber. The sloth bear usually goes out in search of food at night. More than a third of its food supply consists of termites, for which it has developed a highly effective hunting technique. After breaking open the hard termite nest with its sharp claws, the sloth

bear forms a sort of funnel with its extended, trunklike snout. Through this snout, it is able to blow away the dust and eat the insects. The sloth bear's long tongue serves as a sort of "termite fishing pole." The noise it makes while alternately blowing and sucking during a termite meal is often so loud that it can be heard from a distance of almost 220 yards (200 m). The sloth bear also feeds upon dates, mangoes, figs, and other fruits, blossoms, sugarcane, caterpillars, worms, grubs, birds' eggs, and honey.

The sloth bear has no enemies other than people, so it can sleep soundly, unlike most other wild animals. There have occasionally been reports of people out gathering berries or wood who have accidentally awakened a sleeping sloth bear. The sloth bear has then attacked them in panic only because they had come too close and surprised the bear. With its sharp claws and strong canine teeth, the sloth bear is a dangerous opponent who can kill or seriously injure a human being.

After a gestation period of 169 to 210 days, the female sloth bear gives birth to one or two cubs. In northern regions, these cubs are born in December or January. In southern regions, they are born during the warmer months. Mother sloth bears carry their young on their backs. They are the only members of the bear family to do this. The cubs are able to hold on securely to their mother's shaggy fur. They will go out on their own only after two or three years. Then the mother can rejoin her partner.

Unfortunately, sloth bears are threatened with extinction. Their numbers are estimated at only 7,500 to 8,500. In addition, they are still hunted in India. They are either captured to be trained as dancing bears, or killed because of damage they have caused in sugarcane fields.

Opposite: A young sloth bear sits quietly and gazes at its surroundings.

The Sun Bear

Weight: 48-143 pounds (22-65 kg)
Total length: 3-4.6 feet (0.9-1.4 m)

Sun bears are sometimes trained as pets.

The sun bear is the smallest of all the big bears. It lives in tropical zones around the equator from the mainland of Southeast Asia to the islands of Sumatra and Borneo. In some areas, the sun bear is known as the honey bear or Malay bear. Its coat, which is black or dark brown, is short-haired. This short hair keeps the bear comfortable in its warm, tropical climates. It also has a pale yellowish orange, horseshoe-shaped marking on its chest.

The sun bear's front paws are set forward. It has bowed legs and "worry lines" on its forehead. Because of its size and unique features, this bear is often captured while young and trained as a house pet. Even though it doesn't have the same strength as its bigger cousins, the sun bear is still a true bear and should not be regarded merely as a pet. It is excellently adapted to its native habitat in the jungle. With its long, sickle-shaped claws, it is an agile climber and can look for food even in the treetops. In addition to fruit, coconuts, and palm shoots, this bear also likes to eat honey, insects, and small vertebrates. It is good at fishing for ants and termites with its long tongue.

The sun bear moves with great speed across the jungle floor. The type of food that the sun bear eats is spread thinly throughout the jungle. To make up for this scarcity, the sun bear has learned to skim swiftly across the jungle, stopping only briefly to feed.

Since its home is warm throughout the year, the sun bear doesn't usually hibernate. Mating and birthing seasons are not determined by seasons, either. Unlike almost all other bears, sun bears appear to mate for life. The female leaves her mate only to give birth and raise her young. In the protected shelter of a hollow tree or between the roots of a giant tree, she will bring a single cub into the world after a gestation period of 91 to 107 days. This cub is blind when it first opens its eyes. It begins to perceive sounds a week later, and its first teeth come in after eight weeks. At the age of ten weeks, the young sun bear is able to follow its mother, and it begins to climb at fifteen weeks of age.

Sun bears are ready to mate at 3.5 years of age, and they live to be about twenty-five years old. But the sun bear is highly endangered. Its numbers have been decreased by hunting.

Opposite: The sun bear stands easily on its hind legs. It often does this when it senses danger or when it wants to get a clearer view of something far away. The yellow chest markings vary in size from bear to bear.

The Spectacled Bear

Weight: males, 265-440 pounds (120-200 kg);
females, 75-155 pounds (35-70 kg)
Total length: 4-7 feet (1.2-2.1 m)

This bear's "spectacles" are especially bright!

The spectacled bear, also called *ucumari* by the Indian populations in its homeland, is the only bear native to the Southern Hemisphere besides the sun bear. Its territorial range extends from Panama to Argentina. It inhabits the slopes to the east and west of the Andes mountain range, although it can also be seen on the plains as well as in the bleak mountainous regions over 13,000 feet (4,000 m) above sea level. Although the spectacled bear prefers the rain forests between 4,900 and 6,600 feet (1,500-2,000 m) above sea level, it has recently had to compete with people for this habitat. The forested regions have been cleared and converted into farmland at an alarming rate. The spectacled bear has also been hunted for its valuable fur and for the food provided by its meat and fat. Because of these reasons, the numbers of spectacled bears have been severely depleted. The

ucumari that was once protected by the Inca (the Indians who lived in the area before it was invaded by white Europeans) is now rare. In fact, there is an international breeding record book for spectacled bears that is kept at Chicago's Lincoln Park Zoo. Spectacled bears were first born in captivity at a zoo in Buenos Aires, Argentina, on July 9, 1947. Six years later, the zoo in Basel, Switzerland, became the home of the first European-born spectacled bears.

The bears owe their name to the striking, bright marking that often extends from the bridge of the nose and cheeks down to the throat. These "spectacles," which are present at birth and remain unaltered throughout the life of the bear, can be seen on the male bears as well as the smaller females. As a rule, the marking is less distinct on animals that live in the north. But the marking does vary from one animal to the next, making it possible to recognize individual bears by their "spectacles."

Spectacled bears are good climbers that build nests in trees for sleeping. They also like to construct special places in the trees where they can sit and relax during the day. Their food supply consists of figs and other fruits, cacti, palm shoots, plants, corncobs, and insects. Only occasionally do they kill deer, llamas, or, once in a while, small livestock animals. Their voices are distinctive. They don't growl like other bears; they warble. After a gestation period of 150 to 270 days, a female gives birth to one to three cubs. These cubs are always born in the winter, which falls from December to March in the Northern Hemisphere, and from July to September in the Southern Hemisphere.

Opposite: A spectacled bear stands upright in the late afternoon sun. Although these bears look ferocious, they are actually very shy.

The Panda

Weight: 7-22 pounds (3-10 kg)
Total length: 31-44 inches (79-112 cm)

Above: Panda cubs play in a treetop.
Opposite: A panda sits quietly in a dense growth of bamboo.

Zoologists are not certain which animals the panda and the giant panda are related to. Some experts believe that the giant panda is a bear, and that the panda is a relative of the raccoon. Others believe that both are related to raccoons, or that they each constitute their own family group. The panda was once even believed to be a cat and was referred to as the "cat bear." But the panda has nothing at all in common with cats, except the way it bathes. It generously licks its front paw, and then rubs the paw across its face.

In China, the panda is called *hun-he*. This means "fire fox" and refers to the bright reddish coloring on its back. Since its stomach and legs are black, it is among the few mammals that have "reverse coloring." This means that the animal's body is darker underneath than on top.

The panda lives in the mountain forests along the eastern and southeastern slopes of the Himalaya Mountains, where it climbs to heights of over 13,000 feet (4,000 m). With its thick coat and fur-covered soles, it is excellently adapted to the harsh climate. The panda also has sharp claws that help it climb, even though it frequently prefers to stay on the ground. Favorite foods include bamboo and other grasses, roots, berries, and other fruits. The panda sits back on its haunches to eat and brings food to its mouth with its front paws. It occasionally eats insects and small vertebrates such as birds, as well as their eggs. It sleeps in hollow trees or in the forks of trees, and uses its long, bushy tail as a soft pillow.

The panda marks its territory by leaving deposits of vomit in obvious locations. It also "perfumes" its favorite paths with glandular secretions and urine, and uses these scented signals to communicate with other animals. When pandas fight over territory, they sit up on their hind legs and exchange blows.

It is not known if pandas live alone or in pairs. After a gestation period of 114 to 145 days, the female gives birth to usually one or two, but sometimes three or four, cubs. The little ones grow slowly and are carefully kept warm and protected by their mother. After three months, the cubs first come out into the world to play. At about five months of age, they are on their own.

The Giant Panda

Weight: 200-330 pounds (90-150 kg)
Total length: 59-67 inches (1.5-1.7 m)

Above: A mother giant panda gently cuddles her cub while it nurses.
Opposite: A giant panda munches quietly on bamboo, its favorite food.

The Chinese have known the giant panda for centuries. People everywhere have admired its beautiful black and white coat. For many years, China's government allowed the panda out of the country only when it was given as an official state gift. Today, giant pandas are usually lent to zoos only for a few weeks. This is done to provide publicity for protecting this endangered species.

Although the giant panda is a predator, it feeds almost entirely on a few types of bamboo. It mashes the bamboo with its molars, which are more powerful than those of any other predator. The giant panda sits upright to eat and holds the bamboo with the help of a grasping joint that acts as a sixth finger. Since bamboo contains very little nutritional material, the panda must eat 22 to 44 pounds (10-20 kg) of it every day to make it worthwhile.

The giant panda is a loner that needs a territory that covers from 1.5 to 2.7 square miles (4-7 sq km). After a gestation period of 97 to 163 days, the mother gives birth to one or two cubs in August or September. The cubs are born pink and almost hairless.

The giant panda population in the cool, humid mountain forests of the Chinese province of Sichuan is little more than one thousand animals. This animal has been threatened by the destruction of its habitat and by traps that have been set for deer by game hunters. In addition, the types of bamboo that make up its diet bloom only once every 40 to 120 years and then die. This has caused severe problems. In 1970, 138 giant pandas were found dead of starvation.

The Peking Zoo was the first zoo to successfully mate giant pandas in 1963. Since then, only about fifty have been born in captivity, and very few of these have been born outside China. Thanks to the cooperative efforts of the Chinese government and the World Wide Fund for Nature (WWF), the giant panda is now strictly protected.

The Raccoon

Weight: 13-33 pounds (6-15 kg)
Total length: 31-39 inches (80-100 cm)

A young raccoon washes its food carefully in a sparkling stream.

The raccoon is a grayish brown mammal with black cheek patches that make it look like a masked bandit. Its tail is marked with six to seven brownish black rings.

The raccoon is at home in North and Central America, where it prefers to live close to the water. It is a skillful swimmer, and, if near water, always washes its food. In the last few years, the raccoon has been moving farther north, where the climate is milder and where there are more people. This little animal does not shrink back from people but often boldly enters gardens and backyards to rummage through garbage cans.

When it senses danger or just wants to sleep, the raccoon climbs into a hollow tree. Otherwise, it stays on the ground, where it trots along with its head held down and its ringed tail dragging along. The raccoon looks for food on the ground or in the water. With its paws spread wide, it pokes around for food and then rolls it along the ground with its front paws. In this way, it catches insects, earthworms, crabs, snails, mussels, frogs, fish, and small mammals. It will occasionally also find birds' eggs, and it isn't frightened even by the poisonous skins of toads. More than half of a raccoon's diet consists of plant matter such as berries, other fruits, leaves, rinds, corn, and sugarcane. It holds its food tightly in its front paws while eating.

In the fall, acorns that contain fat form the main part of the raccoon's diet. It needs reserves of fat because it loses almost half its body weight during winter. If the temperature sinks below 25°F (-4°C), it retreats to its den and hibernates. It shares its den with several other raccoons.

Raccoons mate in January and February. After a gestation period of sixty-three to sixty-five days, the female gives birth to one to six young. The babies already have the characteristic facial markings at birth. When they are between four and ten months old, the young raccoons go out on their own and often wander as far as 25 miles (40 km) away in order to establish a territory of their own. Females can mate when they are a year old; males must be two years old.

People, pumas, and jaguars are the main enemies of the raccoon. Thanks to their high reproduction rate, raccoons have not become endangered. Most raccoons live to be two to six years old in the wild, while the oldest raccoon in captivity lived to be twenty-two!

The Aquara

Weight: 13-26 pounds (6-12 kg)
Total length: 31-37 inches (80-95 cm)

The aquara's habitat extends from Costa Rica into northern Argentina. This little animal has short, thin hair and is a strong swimmer. The aquara's diet consists almost entirely of crabs and other shellfish, frogs, and fish. Aquaras as well as raccoons are called "wash bears" in Germany. This is because if either the aquara or raccoon is near the water, it will wash its food. If it can't catch its prey in the water, it will carry the prey to the water and roll it around in the water with its front paws to complete the dining ritual.

Mating season for the aquara falls between the months of July and September. The female usually bears two or three young, although sometimes she gives birth to as many as eight babies.

Five smaller types of aquaras live on islands in the Caribbean and off the western coast of Mexico.

Aquaras are at home in tropical climates.

The Cacomistle

Weight: 1.8-2.9 pounds (800-1,300 g)
Total length: 24-41 inches (61-103 cm)

A cacomistle listens carefully to the various sounds around its home.

Cacomistles are the smallest members of the raccoon family and are the only ones able to partly pull their claws back into their paws. The North American cacomistle has big, round ears. It lives in the dry, rocky regions of the western and southwestern United States and in Mexico. The Central American cacomistle has pointed ears and lives in the trees in the rain forests that extend from southern Mexico to Panama. Both types have evolved very little in 50 million years. Their diet consists mostly of small mammals, birds, and eggs in the winter and spring, and insects in summer and fall. Cacomistles locate prey with their keen sense of hearing, stalk it, and pounce. They also like to eat fruit.

After a gestation period of fifty-one to fifty-four days, the female cacomistle gives birth to usually two to four young.

The Kinkajou

Weight: 3-9 pounds (1.4-4.0 kg)
Total length: 32-44 inches (81-113 cm)

The kinkajou can be found in the rain forests from southern Mexico to Brazil. This mammal enjoys its life in the treetops; it is a good climber and can also use its tail to grasp onto branches. It winds its short-haired tail, which is as long as its entire body, around branches and twigs. In this way, it keeps its balance. The kinkajou is the only member of the raccoon family with this sort of prehensile, or grasping, tail.

The kinkajou's mobile, wrinkly skin lies in folds on its forehead. This physical characteristic gives it a unique appearance that many people admire. This little animal is often tamed and kept as a pet.

Kinkajous have glands on their jaw, neck, and belly that produce a musky secretion. Their diet consists of figs, mangoes, avocados, and other fruits that they pick with their teeth or paws. They also love nuts and eggs and will occasionally eat insects. With their narrow, 5-inch- (12-cm-) long tongue, they are able to lick wild honey out of honeycombs for a special treat.

Kinkajous usually live alone or in pairs in the wild. They are nocturnal animals, which means that they are active only at night. During the day, they sleep rolled up in a hollow or fork in a tree. When sleeping, they cover their eyes with their front paws to keep the bright light away.

After a gestation period of 111 to 119 days that has no particular season, the female gives birth to a single baby kinkajou. The mother carries her baby on her neck. At the age of two or three months, the young kinkajou learns how to use its tail to grasp things. At the age of four months it is independent.

A young kinkajou tries to balance itself on a fallen tree limb. It is wrapping its long tail around a small twig. This will help to secure its position to complete the climb.

Males can mate at the age of a year and a half. Females mate only when they are three years old. In the Amsterdam Zoo in the Netherlands, one kinkajou lived to be twenty-three years and seven months old — an astonishing record for this little animal.

The Olingo

Weight: 2-3 pounds (920-1,500 g)
Total length: 30-37 inches (75-95 cm)

Olingos, also known as "slender" or "maki" bears, have been subdivided by zoologists into two groups. One group lives in Central America and northwestern South America, and the other is at home along the upper Amazon. Both are alike in appearance, however, and have almost identical behavioral patterns and habits.

An inhabitant of the tropical rain forest, the olingo, like the kinkajou, is a good climber that lives high in the treetops. Unlike the kinkajou, the olingo's tail is bushy. But the olingo is not able to grasp with its long tail. Instead, its tail is used as a sort of rudder when balancing on thin branches or jumping from branch to branch in leaps of up to 10 feet (3 m). Like the kinkajou, the olingo is also nocturnal, or active at night. It sleeps during the day in hollow trees that it has cushioned with leaves and moss.

Olingos make a wide variety of sounds. They frequently twitter like birds. They can also growl sometimes or screech in high-pitched tones.

Olingos normally live as loners. But if there is a tree with ripe fruit, several olingos can be seen together feasting. Sometimes they are even joined by kinkajous and nocturnal monkeys. Fruit is the main food in the olingo diet. They also eat insects, which they catch by leaping for them, and small mammals. Olingos have big appetites, and they eat about a third of their own body weight every day.

As is usual in the tropics, births take place throughout the year because there is no threat of cold weather or lack of food. The gestation period lasts from seventy-two to seventy-four days. The female olingo bears only one offspring. This baby is usually large and well developed at birth.

The olingo uses its scent glands to ward off enemies by secreting a foul-smelling liquid. Its main enemies are cats such as the ocelot and the jaguarundi, the tayra (a marten), and the boa constrictor.

Almost everything that is known today about the olingo has been learned at the zoo in Louisville, Kentucky. This is the only place, so far, where olingos have been raised in captivity. In the wild, researchers can usually

The soft coat of an olingo can be any color from golden pink to grayish brown. This little fellow is watching cautiously for intruders.

only study the larger animals who live on plains and in deserts and who are active during the day. These kinds of animals are much easier to observe than small animals who are hidden away in the rain forests and only come out at night.

The Red Coati

Weight: 8-12 pounds (3.6-5.4 kg)
Total length: 31-51 inches (80-130 cm)

The red coati has white rings on its tail and whitish coloring on its nose and chest. Its coat is long and thick, and it uses its snout to hunt for food.

Like all members of the raccoon family, the red coati lives in the New World. It lives in the forests of South America from east of the Andes mountain range to northern Argentina and Paraguay. Like raccoons, the red coati has a highly mobile, trunklike nose that it can use to root around for food. It prefers to eat beetles, caterpillars, ants, termites, spiders, scorpions, centipedes, and land crabs. It kills prey by rolling the victim quickly beneath its front paws and will also look for mice and frogs in holes in the ground or sometimes eat fruit. Red coatis will also occasionally eat a bird and its eggs.

In contrast to the rest of the raccoon family, the red coati is an extremely sociable animal that is active during the day. It rolls up in a ball in the fork of a tree at night to sleep. In groups of four to twenty-five animals, the females and their offspring search for food in the forest. While doing so, they twitter and chirp almost constantly and run into the trees if they sense danger. Once in the trees, they artfully balance themselves with their long tails. When the danger is gone, they climb down again headfirst and proceed with their tails held high. The red coatis will take advantage of the interruption to comb each other's fur with their teeth and claws. This routine keeps their coats clean and is a sign of mutual trust.

Male red coatis leave the group at the age of two years and live alone thereafter. One single male will join up with a group of females at mating time. After a gestation period of sixty-eight to seventy-seven days, the female gives birth between April and June to two to five young.

Researchers know next to nothing about another relative of the red coati, the "small" or "mountain" coati. This little animal lives in the mountain forests of northern South America. It weighs only 7 pounds (3 kg) and is 28 to 31 inches (70-80 cm) long.

The Coati

Weight: 10-24 pounds (4.5-11 kg)
Total length: 39-53 inches (100-135 cm)

What is true of the red coati is also true of its close relative, the coati. Coatis are sociable animals that are active during the day. But while the red coatis are almost exclusively forest dwellers, the coatis also feel at home in open grasslands and in dry, desertlike areas. They inhabit the dry areas from Ecuador to Colombia west of the Andes mountain range, extending over Panama and as far north as the southwestern United States. In Arizona, New Mexico, and Texas, it sometimes gets so cold that the tips of the coatis' tails freeze.

Male coatis tend to live alone. But the territory of a group of females is usually about 100 acres (40 ha), and they sometimes overlap. If there is a tree with ripe fruit in the area, several groups will gather together to enjoy the abundance.

In the females' territories, there will always be a few lone males. They join the females only during the mating season, between January and March. Often the males fight one another for the favors of the females. After a gestation period of seventy-four days, the females leave the group to give birth to baby coatis. Mothers give birth in a den in the ground or a nest in a tree. The young leave the nest after three or four weeks, but the mother brings them back for a longer amount of time. The females carry their young by the scruff of the neck. After five weeks, the mothers will rejoin the group with their young. The babies are able to fend for themselves after a few more weeks, although they must nurse for four months. Coatis are ready to mate at two years of age. If a group gets too large, it will split up into smaller groups.

Aside from the puma, jaguar, and boa constrictor, the coati has only people to fear. It is often hunted for meat, and young coatis are often captured in North America as pets.

A young coati snuggles comfortably into the fork of a tree.

The "Bear" That Isn't a Bear:

The Koala

Weight: 9-30 pounds (4-13.5 kg)
Total length: 24-32 inches (60-82 cm)

A mother koala and her baby go out on their daily search for food.

At first glance, the koala's soft coat, furry ears, and dark nose remind people of a teddy bear. Because of this, the koala is frequently called the "koala bear" or "marsupial bear." But the koala really has little in common with bears. Like the kangaroo and the wombat, it is a marsupial. Its habits are much more like those of opossums or sloths.

Millions of koalas once lived in the eucalyptus forests of Australia. But their numbers have been greatly reduced by the destruction of their habitats by human settlement. These forests are often cleared by fire and disease. Koalas have also suffered from Aboriginals, who hunted with boomerangs, and white hunters with guns. In 1924 alone, two million koala pelts were sold on the market. The beautiful marsupials were finally legally protected in 1927. Today, there are still koalas along the coast of eastern Australia and in the state of South Australia.

Outside of Australia, however, koalas can only be seen in zoos. This is because they are difficult to feed. Koalas eat only eucalyptus leaves, and only 6 of the 350 types of eucalyptus are appropriate for them. Also, eucalyptus leaves are poisonous at certain times of year and in certain stages of growth. This makes the food supply even smaller.

Koalas sleep for about eighteen hours a day in the forks of trees. They spend the rest of the time slowly looking for food in the treetops. Since they have two "thumbs" on each of their front paws as well as one on each hind paw, they are very good at navigating their way through branches and twigs. Koalas rarely have to drink because eucalyptus leaves contain large amounts of water. In fact, the name *koala* means "doesn't drink" in the language of the native population.

Koalas are loners and come together only to mate. After a gestation period of thirty-four to thirty-six days, the female gives birth to just one baby. The baby koala, like the baby kangaroo, is small enough to fit in a teaspoon. Unlike the kangaroo, the koala's pouch opens toward the back. After about five months, the baby koala can drink a sort of predigested eucalyptus porridge directly from the mother's intestine, as well as the mother's milk. This special feeding system to nourish the baby in the pouch is one of the many wonders of nature. At the age of six months, the baby leaves the pouch to be carried on its mother's back like a backpack. The baby koala goes out on its own when it is a year old.

Opposite: Koalas have a large head and nose and big, furry ears.

Every Child's Favorite:
The Teddy Bear

The teddy bear is one of the world's favorite toys. The most believable and most popular story of its development was told by a German stuffed-toy manufacturer named Richard Steiff. Steiff made a little plush bear with moving arms and legs in 1902 and presented it at the Leipzig Toy Convention a year later. At about the same time, U.S. president Theodore Roosevelt went on a bear-hunting expedition. He wasn't having much luck when he finally spotted a young bear through his sights. The president hesitated to shoot the little fellow and let him return to his mother. From then on, U.S. cartoonist Clifton Berryman always drew President "Teddy" Roosevelt with a small bear — "Teddy's bear!" When the president's daughter married in 1906, stuffed bears from the Steiff firm decorated the tables, and the teddy bear was born. It became so popular that almost a million were sold in that year alone. Since then, millions of the plushy, soft teddy bears have appeared in children's rooms and in their hearts the world over.

APPENDIX TO ANIMAL FAMILIES

BEARS
and their forest cousins

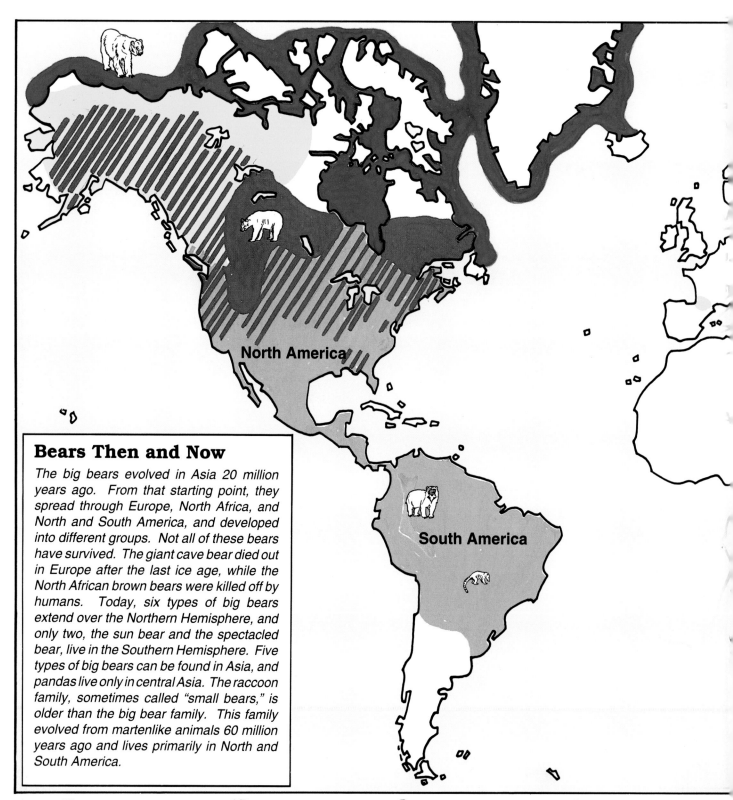

Bears Then and Now

The big bears evolved in Asia 20 million years ago. From that starting point, they spread through Europe, North Africa, and North and South America, and developed into different groups. Not all of these bears have survived. The giant cave bear died out in Europe after the last ice age, while the North African brown bears were killed off by humans. Today, six types of big bears extend over the Northern Hemisphere, and only two, the sun bear and the spectacled bear, live in the Southern Hemisphere. Five types of big bears can be found in Asia, and pandas live only in central Asia. The raccoon family, sometimes called "small bears," is older than the big bear family. This family evolved from martenlike animals 60 million years ago and lives primarily in North and South America.

North America

South America

Brown bears

Black bears

Polar bears

Himalayan black bears

Pandas

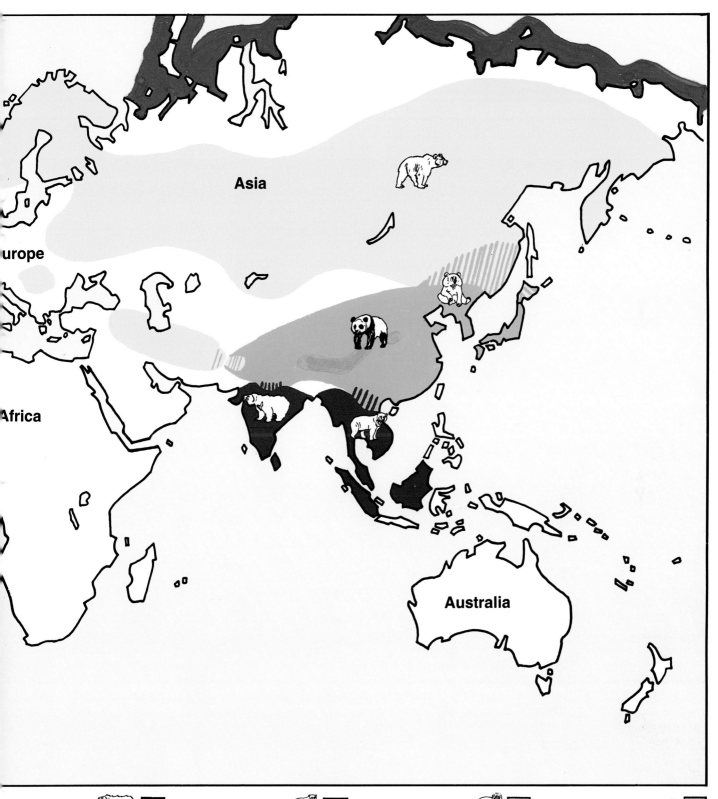

Asia

Europe

Africa

Australia

Sloth bears

Sun bears

Spectacled bears

Raccoons

ABOUT THESE BOOKS

Although this series is called "Animal Families," these books aren't just about fathers, mothers, and young. They also discuss the scientific definition of *family*, which is a division of biological classification and includes many animals.

Biological classification is a method that scientists use to identify and organize living things. Using this system, scientists place animals and plants into larger groups that share similar characteristics. Characteristics are physical features, natural habits, ancestral backgrounds, or any other qualities that make one organism either like or different from another.

The method used today for biological classification was introduced in 1753 by a Swedish botanist-naturalist named Carolus Linnaeus. Although many scientists tried to find ways to classify the world's plants and animals, Linnaeus's system seemed to be the only useful choice. Charles Darwin, a famous British naturalist, referred to Linnaeus's system in his theory of evolution, which was published in his book *On the Origin of Species* in 1859. Linnaeus's system of classification, shown below, includes seven major categories, or groups. These are: kingdom, phylum, class, order, family, genus, and species.

An easy way to remember the divisions and their order is to memorize this sentence: "Ken Put Cake On Frank's Good Shirt." The first letter of each word in this sentence gives you the first letter of a division. (The *K* in *Ken*, for example, stands for *kingdom*.) The order of the words in this sentence gives the order of the divisions from largest to smallest. The kingdom is the largest of these divisions; the species is the smallest. The larger the division, the more types of animals or plants it contains. For example, the animal kingdom, called Animalia, contains everything from worms to whales. Smaller divisions, such as the family, have fewer members that share more characteristics. For example, members of the bear family, Ursidae, include the polar bear, the brown bear, and many others.

In the following chart, the lion species is followed through all seven categories. As the categories expand to include more and more members, remember that only a few examples are pictured here. Each division has many more members.

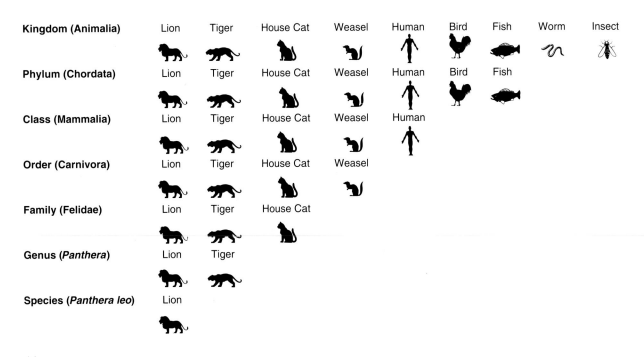

	Lion	Tiger	House Cat	Weasel	Human	Bird	Fish	Worm	Insect
Kingdom (Animalia)	Lion	Tiger	House Cat	Weasel	Human	Bird	Fish	Worm	Insect
Phylum (Chordata)	Lion	Tiger	House Cat	Weasel	Human	Bird	Fish		
Class (Mammalia)	Lion	Tiger	House Cat	Weasel	Human				
Order (Carnivora)	Lion	Tiger	House Cat	Weasel					
Family (Felidae)	Lion	Tiger	House Cat						
Genus (*Panthera*)	Lion	Tiger							
Species (*Panthera leo*)	Lion								

SCIENTIFIC NAMES OF THE ANIMALS IN THIS BOOK

Animals have different names in every language. For this reason, researchers the world over use the same scientific names, which usually stem from ancient Greek or Latin. Most animals are classified by two names. One is the genus name; the other is the name of the species to which they belong. Additional names indicate further subgroupings. Here is a list of the animals included in *Bears and Their Forest Cousins*.

Big Bears

European brown bear .... *Ursus arctos arctos*
Grizzly bear .... *Ursus arctos horribilis*
Kodiak bear .... *Ursus arctos middendorffi*
Syrian brown bear .... *Ursus arctos syriacus*
American black bear .... *Ursus americanus americanus*
Cinnamon bear .... *Ursus americanus cinnamomum*
Glacier bear .... *Ursus americanus emmonsii*
Kermode bear .... *Ursus americanus kermodei*
Polar bear .... *Thalarctos maritimus*
Himalayan black bear .... *Selenarctos thibetanus*
Sloth bear .... *Melursus ursinus*
Sun bear .... *Helarctos malayanus*
Spectacled bear .... *Tremarctos ornatus*

Pandas

Giant panda .... *Ailuropoda melanoleuca*
Panda .... *Ailurus fulgens*

Raccoons

Raccoon ....*Procyon lotor*
Aquara .... *Procyon cancrivorus*
North American cacomistle .... *Bassariscus astutus*
Central American cacomistle ..... *Bassariscus sumichrasti*
Kinkajou ....*Potos flavus*
Central American olingo .... *Bassaricyon gabbii*
South American olingo .... *Bassaricyon alleni*
Red coati .... *Nasua nasua*
Coati .... *Nasua narica*

GLOSSARY

botanist
A person who studies plants.

carnivore
A predominantly meat-eating animal.

class
The third of seven divisions in the biological classification system proposed by Swedish botanist-naturalist Carolus Linnaeus. The class is the main subdivision of the phylum. Bears belong to the class Mammalia. Animals in this class, which includes humans, share some features: they have skin covered with hair, they give birth to live young, and they nourish their young with milk from mammary glands.

cub
A baby bear. Bear cubs are very small and completely helpless at birth.

den
A shelter, such as a cave, for wild animals.

eucalyptus
An evergreen tree with strong-smelling leaves that is found mostly in Australia. Koalas eat only eucalyptus leaves, so it is sometimes difficult to find food for them.

evolution
The gradual process of change that occurs in any organism and its descendants over a long period of time. Organisms evolve in order to survive the changes that can occur in climate, food supply, air quality, and other such factors.

family
The fifth of seven divisions in the biological classification system proposed by Swedish botanist-naturalist Carolus Linnaeus. The family is the main subdivision of the order and contains one or more genera. Bears belong to the family Ursidae.

genus (plural: **genera**)
The sixth of seven divisions in the biological classification system proposed by Swedish botanist-

naturalist Carolus Linnaeus. A genus is the main subdivision of a family and includes one or more species. The bears in this book belong to several different genera.

gestation period
The number of days from actual conception to the birth of an animal. Gestation periods vary greatly for different types of animals.

glacier
A flat body of ice that spreads across valleys or other large areas of land.

habitat
An area or environment in which an animal usually lives. Many bear habitats have been invaded and settled by humans.

hemisphere
One of the two halves, either north or south, into which the earth is divided by the equator.

herbivore
An animal whose diet consists mainly of plants. Some biologists and other experts believe that the Himalayan black bear is a herbivore.

hibernation
A period of time, usually in the winter, during which an animal goes into a deep sleep. Although bears are not true hibernators, many species sleep for long periods of time in winter.

kingdom
The first of seven divisions in the biological classification system proposed by Swedish botanist-naturalist Carolus Linnaeus. Animals, including humans, belong to the kingdom Animalia. It is one of five kingdoms.

marsupial
A species of mammals in which the female shelters her young in an external abdominal pouch until fully developed. Koala bears are examples of marsupials.

naturalist
A person who studies and observes plants and animals in their natural setting.

nocturnal
Active at night; usually asleep during the day. Kinkajous and olingos are examples of nocturnal animals.

omnivore
An animal that eats both animal and plant substances. Brown bears are examples of omnivorous animals.

order
The fourth of seven divisions in the biological classification system proposed by Swedish botanist-naturalist Carolus Linnaeus. The order is the main subdivision of the class and usually contains many different families. Bears, for example, belong to the order known as Carnivora. This order is shared by other meat-eating animal families such as dogs, cats, hyenas, weasels, and others.

phylum (plural: phyla)
The second of seven divisions in the biological classification system proposed by Swedish botanist-naturalist Carolus Linnaeus. A phylum is one of the main divisions of a kingdom. Bears belong to the phylum Chordata, the group consisting mainly of animals with backbones (vertebrates).

predator
An animal that lives by eating other animals. The Kodiak bear is the largest land predator on earth.

prehensile
Adapted for holding or wrapping around an object. Kinkajous have prehensile tails that they often use to establish balance.

prey
Any creature hunted or caught as food. Insects, crabs, frogs, and fish are often prey for the raccoon.

species
The last of seven divisions in the biological classification system proposed by Swedish botanist-naturalist Carolus Linnaeus. The species is the main subdivision of the genus. It may include further subgroups of its own, called subspecies. At the level of species, members share many features and are capable of breeding with one another.

MORE BOOKS ABOUT BEARS

The Amazing World of Animals (3 vols.). (Grolier)
Bears. Jane Heath Buxton (National Geographic Society)
Bears. Bernard Stonehouse (Wayland)
Bears in the Wild. Ada Graham and Frank Graham (Delacorte)
The Black Bear. Mark Ahlstrom (Crestwood House)
The Black Bear Book. Joe Van Wormer (Caxton)
A Closer Look at Bears and Pandas. Bibby Whittaker (Franklin Watts)
Grizzly Country. Andy Russell (Knopf)
The Polar Bear. Mark Ahlstrom (Crestwood House)
The Polar Bear on the Ice. Martin Banks (Gareth Stevens)
Seven True Bear Stories. Laura Geriner (Hastings)

PLACES TO WRITE

The following are some of the many organizations that exist to educate people about animals, promote the protection of animals, and encourage the conservation of their environments. Write to these organizations for more information about bears, other animals, or animal concerns of interest to you. When you write, include your name, address, and age, and tell them clearly what you want to know. Don't forget to enclose a stamped, self-addressed envelope for a reply.

Animal Protection Institute
P.O. Box 22505
Sacramento, California 95822

Canadian Wildlife Federation
1673 Carling Avenue, Suite 203
Ottawa, Ontario K2A 3Z1

Student Action Corps for Animals
P.O. Box 15588
Washington, D.C. 20003

People for the Ethical Treatment of
    Animals (PETA)
P.O. Box 42516
Washington, D.C. 20015

Elsa Clubs of America
P.O. Box 4572
North Hollywood, California
              91617-0572

Wildlife Preservation Trust International
34th Street and Girard Avenue
Philadelphia, Pennsylvania 19104

THINGS TO DO

These projects are designed to help you have fun with what you've learned about bears. You can do them alone, in small groups, or as a class project.

1. Have a contest between individuals or teams: Write down the names of as many bears as you can remember from history, fairy tales and other stories, and television programs and movies (Examples: Winnie-the-Pooh, Smokey Bear, The Three Bears, Yogi Bear, Paddington). Can you identify what kind of bear each is supposed to be?

2. Visit a local zoo and see how many of the bears from this book you can identify. Draw or paint a picture of your favorite bear.

3. Look at a map or globe and see if you can identify in which part of the world each bear species mentioned in this book can be found in nature.

INDEX

adaptation 11, 16, 17, 24
Alp bears 15
American black bears 10, 16
aquaras 10, 33
Atlas bears 8

bamboo 30
bears: gestation periods of 16, 22, 24, 26; history
    of 7-8; mating habits of 12, 15, 16, 18, 24
biological classification 44
black bears 8, 16-17
brown bears 7, 11-15

cacomistles 10, 33
camouflage 18
cave bears 7
cinnamon bears 10, 17
coatis 10, 37 (*see also* red coatis)

Darwin, Charles 44
dens 9, 12, 18, 32, 37

endangered species 22, 24, 30
eucalyptus 38
European brown bears 8, 10, 11-12

giant pandas 10, 28, 30-31
glacier bears 10, 17
grizzly bears 7, 8, 10, 13

habitats 8, 11, 15, 16, 17, 20, 24, 26, 30, 33
hibernation 9, 12, 16, 18, 20, 32
Himalayan black bears 10, 20-21
Hornaday, William T. 17

Kermode, Francis 17
Kermode bears 10, 17
kinkajous 10, 34
koalas 38-39
Kodiak bears 7, 10, 14-15

Linnaeus, Carolus 44, 45, 46

livestock 15, 20, 26

mammals: evolution of bears from 7; as prey 16, 18,
    32, 33
marsupials 38
mating habits 12, 15, 16, 18, 24, 32, 33, 36, 37, 38
miacids 7
mountain coatis 36

naturalists 17
nocturnal animals 34, 35

olingos 10, 35

pandas 10, 28-29 (*see also* giant pandas)
pelts 17, 38
polar bears 8, 10, 18-19
predators 8, 15, 30
Protursus 7

raccoon family: gestation periods of 32, 33, 34, 35,
    36, 37; mating habits of 32, 33, 34, 36, 37
raccoons 10, 32
red coatis 10, 36, 37
reverse coloring 28

sloth bears 8, 10, 22-23
spectacled bears 8, 10, 26-27
sun bears 10, 24-25
Syrian brown bears 10, 15

teddy bears 40
territories 11, 16, 37
tundra 11

vertebrates (as prey) 24, 28 (*see also* mammals:
    as prey)

zoologists 28, 35